LIMITED edition, 2019

©2019 Sara Farish & Ayn Gailey

All rights reserved. This book or parts thereof may not be reproduced in any form, stored in any retrieval system, or transmitted in any form by any means—electronic, mechanical, photocopy, recording, or otherwise—without prior written permission from the publisher, except in the case of brief quotations embodied in reviews and certain other noncommercial uses permitted by copyright law. For permission requests contact the publishers at the addresses below.

info@odeislove.com
www.odeislove.com

St. Ōde Press
PO Box 370
Eastsound, Washington 98245

ISBN: 978-0-578-60473-2
Library of Congress C.N.:2019918069

Printed in Vancouver, B.C.

Cover credits:
Cedar goat mask by Rivkah Sweedler & Walter H. Barkas II
Wood block photo by AJ Ragasa
Other photos by Ayn Gailey

Opening page photo by Peter Lin Carrillo
Hand-painted fabrics by Sara Farish

Book + Cover Design by Sara Farish & Ayn Gailey

ŌDE
www.odeislove.com

St. Ōde Press prints 100% Carbon Neutral on Forest-Positive, FSC paper

ŌDE

For all those who love this place we call home. To all those souls who came before us and all who will come after.

A lyric poem usually marked by exaltation
of feeling and style, varying length of line,
and complexity of stanza forms.

WIND & SEA

48.6967
122.9061

EASTSOUND, WASHINGTON, U.S.A.

There once was a young island girl who loved an island boy. In the summer they floated on driftwood in the sea. When she had to leave, she gave him a Mason jar of water and whispered to him, "In this jar is the rain and the ocean and the sea. As long as you have it, you'll always have a part of me."

The girl knew that as the water above us and around us and beneath us is connected in intricate ways, so, too, are we. The name Salish Sea pays homage to the Coast Salish first peoples who have lived on the shores of the waters we call home for thousands upon thousands of years.

Lured by the Sea

Words by Toby Cooper | Photographs by Dennis DeHart

All the while, wind, sea and sky conspire to shape your daily mood, your appetite for movement, your hunger for humanity.

Tiffany Loney sits on her cottage deck stripping dried leaves from Lemon Balm stems into a pail at her feet. Spread before the deck is a priceless inventory of nature's scenic offerings: distant shores of two nations, a fascination of sky and clouds, sea with whitecaps, and a splendor of green islands begging for attention. The rhythm of her task allows frequent glances at the stunning panorama, feeding her soul as a hummingbird seeks constant nectar.

"We ran wild as kids," she offers, referring to the unfettered freedoms enjoyed by certain lucky youngsters. She recalls how she and her sisters scampered between households on backwoods paths, blind to the confines of property lines. They discovered the essence of island life. They savored wild blackberries. They grew up on Orcas.

Red hair rolled back in a bun, she fleetingly channels a self-sufficient pioneer living off the land. The newly-stripped twigs of the lemon-scented mint, bundled like makeshift brooms, pile on the deck, merging with bleached driftwood, burnished beach glass, pebbles, and other assembled trophies of beach-front life. The picture is complete. It is at once simple, tranquil, vibrant, and authentic, a fitting metaphor for this tiny corner of the sprawling nation known as America.

Orcas Island. The very name conjures up mysteries of the deep. It is a place in some ways forgotten in time. Orcas nurtures those who come. Orcas heals. Orcas seduces, but gently, with promises of solitude. But what fortuitous twist of fate brought this humble family, now three generations strong, to an island with all that magic? For this, simply slide back to a foggy winter's day nearly a half-century ago.

By early December 1975, OPEC's oil market manipulations had pitched the Western World into recession, Bill Gates and Paul Allen had named their fledgling startup "Micro-Soft," and Brenda and Barry Loney had decided on a weekend getaway to Orcas Island. As distant markets festered, the Loney's Canadian dollars gained fortuitous new clout in the U.S., and that meant a certain Raccoon Point property was thrown on the market at a fire-sale price.

Buying property had not been on the weekend agenda. "Oh, let's go take a look," they had said, "just for fun." But they never expected to fall in love so quickly. Brenda stood on the tiny deck of the tuck box cabin and let its seaside ambiance soak into her soul. She turned to Barry, hoping to resolve the swelling panic of indecision, mentally shuffling and reshuffling bank balances and assets, hopes, dreams, and those elusive fantasy wish lists young couples never quite unload. But it was no use. Barry mirrored it all right back, and for the moment they stalemated.

"We can't," she heard Barry saying. However, Brenda, it seemed, could not let go. Within mere hours bank balances did get shuffled, hopes and dreams became thoroughly rechanneled, and "we can't" became "we did." Overnight, the Loneys established an island toehold that would change their lives forever.

Their new hand-hewn wooden cabin was actually one of several humble structures on what had been one man's recession-sidelined vision for a modest seaside resort. In the Loney's eyes, it effortlessly morphed into a diminutive compound for a growing family.

And so it began. Brenda and Barry soon felt their feet become one with the land. Their spirits blended with the welcoming Orcas community where wind, sea, and sky conspire to shape your daily mood, your appetite for movement, your hunger for humanity.

Days became years and years became decades. They welcomed four daughters: Jane, Alison, Jennifer, and the youngest, Tiffany. Brenda reveled in song, taught herself dance, and marveled as her artistry flourished spontaneously in all of her girls. The sea beckoned, so they sailed, sometimes for months. They shuttled to Canada for part of each year but always came back. Brenda anchored the family and the family anchored to the land, to the magic of Orcas.

"The sea taught our family to move as a unit."

Tiffany pauses in her reflections as a gull yelps overhead. An Orcas wind toys with her hair, or does her hair toy with the wind? She is no stranger to wind. Tiffany and husband Bruce Halabisky circled the planet, consuming eleven glorious years on their handsome Atkin gaff cutter. Wind was their companion, their pleasure, their fear, their treasure. "At sea, your life is completely dictated by the elements," she smiles knowingly. "Your moods change with it. You learn patience. You observe every detail of that timeless ocean, and if you tried to fight it, you would go crazy." To Tiffany and Bruce, above all else, sailing is honest.

Tiffany was born with her mother's innate talent for dance—she began at five, retired at nine, and staged a comeback at ten for good. For a dancer who feasts on simulated flight, the transition to life on a small boat should have been stifling but instead proved exhilarating. At ports across the South Pacific, she conducted classes in dance and yoga just as she does now on Orcas Island. She marveled at how the perpetual motion of the sea itself supplied endless inspiration. "You have to surrender to it," she says, gazing at the stand of leathery salal growing beyond Brenda's deck. "Your world moves endlessly and you flow with it. Stepping off the boat does not end the flow."

The boat was their universe. When children arrived, the boat became the schoolhouse for lessons much of the world never quite learns. As Tiffany speaks, Solianna and Seffa, 12 and 8, crawl into her circle. Solianna was born in New Zealand, Seffa in Victoria, both well before the return to land. Seffa's first toddling steps were memorably taken with the boat secured in a Maine cove during Hurricane Irene. With the arrival of the girls, Tiffany and Bruce began to feel the pull of shore-side life. As Tiffany puts it: "Terra Firma—nothing quite like it!" And, so, after a generous decade of adventure at sea, Orcas beckoned them back.

Not a day passes that Tiffany does not marvel at certain gifts that life has provided. "The sea taught our family to move as a unit," she reveals, adding that when weather threatened, "Soli knew the order to secure little Seffa. She followed procedures without question. Out there, you are always part of a team."

> "Brenda anchored the family and the family anchored to the land, to the magic of Orcas."

During our last interview, we watch as Soli, with her hefty cello, and Seffa, with her violin, head for the local Farmers' Market, where they plan to perform with a friend as a seraphic trio of street musicians, violin case set agape to welcome donations. "They do well," says Tiffany, "This is Orcas after all."

Brenda sits facing seaward, her back symbolically turned to the inexorable creep of change on her beloved island. Hammers bang in the distance as a new structure rises in a stand of fir. Old Orcas inevitably gives way to the new. Brenda tolerates change if it comes in small doses and settles harmoniously into the landscape. She admires Tiffany, though, who is inclined to speak up where she can, wishing to save something of the Old before it is lost.

But what of Soli and Seffa? What kind of island will they inherit? Would they chase the illusion of progress and opportunity on the mainland? "Never," Tiffany opines. "They have a different baseline. Today's Orcas is what they know, and what they know is a magical place that sets you free."

When slack comes, it blankets the narrows in magical stillness. It's as if a window, once closed and shuttered, has been flung open and another world lets itself be seen. Tension dissolves. Short breaths become long. A fish jumps; two cormorants take flight, stretching their slender black bodies across the narrows.

From *Tides—The Science and Spirit of the Ocean* by Jonathan White
Photo by Deborah Heffley Jones

"Growing up on island means...there are no secrets."

When my dad died, I wanted to isolate myself completely, but this community wouldn't have it. In a big city, I believe my story would have fallen through the cracks in the sidewalk.

Words by Flora Lister — In Loving Memory of Ian Lister
Photographs by Peter Lin Carrillo

Anthropocene Sketchbook

Anthropocene is an informal geologic term referring to the period that began when the human impact on the world's ecosystems first became significant.

Artist and biologist Robin Lee Carlson's family has been visiting Orcas Island for decades. This summer, we invited Robin and her six-year-old son, Isaac, to hike Cascade Creek from Mountain Lake to the San Juan County Land Bank's Coho Preserve. While Isaac sketched stained glass windows (his current obsession) purely from imagination, Robin documented their journey and a complex ecosystem with her field drawings. See her full sketchbook at odeislove.com.

nodding onion
Allium cernuum

just at the edge of the rocky beach

Buck Bay where Cascade Creek exits to the sea & where Buck Bay Shellfish Farm grows oysters and clams

mouth of Cascade Creek

broken shells on the beach:
pacific oyster
    Crassostrea gigas
Manila clam
    Venerupis philippinarum

The Art of Getting Lost

When you lived in the City, you liked thinking about the vault. You often pictured it, built into the side of an icy mountain, on an island floating far above the arctic circle, shrouded in absolute silence. You found the thought of it calm-inducing, even though its nickname is The Doomsday Vault. Scientists claim its contents will make it possible to restart humankind after a global crisis of apocalyptic proportions, yet the vault does not contain weapons, intelligence data, or medicines. Nor does it contain the items you personally would want to help you survive an apocalypse: your favorite pair of sweatpants, your record collection, your Chinese grandmother's recipes. The vault contains seeds, 930,000 varieties of seeds for plants whose fiber can be consumed or worn. The vault, in essence, is a plan to ensure that those who survive will be able to feed and clothe themselves.

You were always drawn to this idea of a back-up plan of these proportions. It meant that no matter how badly we humans mess things up—and boy, do we show a propensity for that—we can start over.

The last time you started over it was 2015. You, and your man, and your child traveled to the San Juan Islands on a whim. You marveled at the giant ferry that ushered you through an archipelago that felt like you were heading to unchartered waters—in a way you were. After decades of living in Los Angeles, you couldn't remember the last time you felt the wind in your hair. You tried—and failed— to contain your excitement the first time you tasted a Brown Bear *croissant abricot*; you were in humble disbelief at the simple unattended farm stand that trusted you to leave your money and make your own change; and, the first time you walked into the old chapel behind the Outlook Inn, the sunlight streaming through stained glass windows, you breathed in the scent of the wooden pews, and your soul let out a deep sigh.

Still, you couldn't imagine tossing out your life plans, and their accompanying back-up plans, and leaving the once-beloved city that had been your home for 25 years. But, as often happens on the island, despite worries and obstacles, events conspire in one's favor—whether you know it or not at the time. For you, that meant your third day on the island and a cab dropping you off at Catkin Café. How could you possibly know that a café would be closed during the height of summer on a weekday? You may have panicked slightly when you couldn't get reception to make a call to tell your family where to pick you up. So, you set out on foot, in search of a landline.

You had no idea where you were or where you were going. You were lost—a feeling you had not experienced in many years. As you set out with nowhere in mind, you came within a few feet of the first bald eagle you'd ever seen outside of a zoo. You plucked a wild blackberry from a wicked vine and delighted at its sweet-sour flesh. You spotted a sign for clams at a place called Buck Bay Shellfish. You didn't know then that you'd come back to this spot many times in the future—as an islander. The owner let you use the phone—the weight of its long coiled cord reminding you of a simpler time—then she set you up at a picnic table with a tray of steamed Dungeness crab and fresh tomatoes straight from her garden. As you cracked open the crab, you watched her collect people's discarded clam and crab shells and deliver them right back to the sea. You felt the wind tug at your hair (or was it your heart?). You watched the tide ebb, and you yearned to watch it return. And, when your husband came to find you, you told him that you realized that losing your way may have been the best thing to happen to you in a long time. He looked at you with a contented grin and said, "I know. I was lost, too."

Words and images by Ayn Gailey

Approximate Dreams

Words by Samuel W. Gailey | Photographs by Dennis DeHart

A two-year plan and a dream become a thirty-year odyssey with a little help from friends and neighbors.

Nestled deep in the woods of Mt. Pickett, six miles from the closest viable boat launch—six miles down steep, narrow dirt roads riddled with switchbacks and trees—lies a slowly deteriorating, eighty-foot-long, fifty-ton ship. The ship is known as Aproximada, and it is the ephemeral remnant of a seemingly unfathomable dream by Orcas Islander App Applegate.

In the 1970s, Applegate, a retired physics and chemistry professor, began crafting the three-masted barkentine sailing vessel from Douglas firs on his own property. While most ships this size are built by a team of a hundred, App began his endeavor alone, designing Aproximada almost entirely by mathematics without blueprints. App relied solely on a hand calculator and reams of paper. And, what started as a project that in App's words, would be done in two years, became a thirty-year odyssey. His ultimate dream was to launch from Obstruction Pass one day and sail to Cuba.

Some might ask why someone, anyone, would decide to build a ship on an island in the middle of the woods at four hundred feet above sea level without knowing how the vessel would be transported to the coastal waterways. These factors never deterred App. In fact, even as the years then decades crawled past, this man (barely five-feet tall), never outgrew his idealism.

After word spread on the island that App was constructing the ship by himself, islanders showed up at his Mt. Pickett property, asking the simple question: Can I help? No one was ever turned away. Instead, they were invited aboard the Aproximada, treated to coffee and stories, and, yes, put to work. App's longtime companion, Rivkah Sweedler, who enjoyed what she refers to as shared-solitude with App for almost two decades, reflects fondly upon her time with him, "The journey was not the planned trip to launch and sail the ship. The real journey was the actual experience of working with App."

In an era where the path of least resistance and shortcuts are preferred, App's story truly stands out. App and the Aproximada are reminders that we create our own world by the way we choose to see it, and that there is power in perseverance. In the end, for those neighbors who worked side-by-side with the shipbuilder until his death at the age of 94, there were no regrets that the Aproximada never sailed the Salish Sea. Being a part of App Applegate's dream was never about building a ship—it was about helping a neighbor build a dream.

Learn more about App Applegate and his dream by exploring the Orcas Island Film Festival winning short, "Aproximada," by Kyle Carver & Dan Larson

The journey was not the planned trip to launch and sail the ship.

48°38'38.01"N 122°47'55.40"W

The real journey was the actual experience of working with App.

— Rivkah Sweedler

Painter Martha Farish

*Martha Farish ruminates on her journey
as a painter and her ongoing collaboration
with with place, beauty, and light.*

One never knows where the conversation might lead when you sit down to talk to artist Martha Farish. The first time we spoke, we wept, or at least I did, about children growing up and away, about immortality, and about the cycles of life, and Nirvana, not the band with ties to islander Bruce Pavitt, but the spiritual state when one is released from the cycle of death and rebirth.

Today we're talking about the color purple, and Martha knows Smithsonian-level details on the history of the color once reserved for royalty. When Martha first used the color purple in painting, it was almost twenty years ago, she was at the beginning of her painter's journey at age fifty, and she was living in Southern California. "California light is yellow, and the complement to that is purple," she explains. "But purple is complex. And, historically, it was hard to come by, which is one reason it was reserved for royalty in ancient times. To make even a few grams of purple dye, it took tens of thousands of marine snails, boiled for days in giant lead vats." Side note: The snails were not actually purple to begin with. Craftsmen harvested chemical precursors from the snails that, once exposed to heat and light, were transformed into the valuable dye known then as Tyrian purple.

When Martha explains that "purple was and is a transitional color," she means in more ways than one. In the Victorian era it was the color that etiquette encouraged a woman to wear after she wore black for two years to mourn the death of a loved one. This period was referred to as half-mourning. "Visually, purple gets you from one extreme to another in painting, or from one awkward shape to another awkward shape. When I painted *Origins*, I was learning about shadows being a shade of purple, even though my mind was trying to tell me they were darker grey to blackish." This doesn't seem like a big deal, but Martha reminds me that it wasn't until the Impressionists that painters started to use colors other than shades of black to convey shadows.

First painting: *Purpurus Abstractus*, oil on canvas, 24 x 30
Second painting: *Quincunx*, oil on canvas, 48 x 60
Third painting: *Woman on Horizon*, oil on canvas, 36 x 36, painted for Sara Farish on Orcas Island

In 2005, after a lifetime of visiting Orcas Island, Martha and her husband, Joseph Cohen, a financial advisor and avid kayaker (they actually met when Martha was two-years-old) became full-time Orcas residents. When their permanent address changed, Martha's painting style changed, too.

"In California, I was painting in a city, which meant I was always painting a contained vista. On Orcas, every time I turned right, I was struck by an expanse of color, of sea and of sky. I started to paint more horizons, and continued to use purple to transition between more blues, greens, and greys." Her large scale painting entitled *Quincunx* is a perfect example of her style expanding along with her environment. The painting is a beautiful depiction of the vista from her home on Fishing Bay. Martha has also started to paint more abstracts, including her *360° Series*, which can be viewed on her website accompanied by music from Orcas Island musicians, Stephen Fairweather, Mandy Troxel, Michael Grady, and Paris Wilson. For her, abstractionism was a reaction to the immense beauty of Orcas Island.

> "Trying to capture an exact representation of our surroundings on Orcas Island feels futile, almost disrespectful. There's no way I will match its beauty, but I can occasionally collaborate with it."

As our conversation comes to a close, we circle back to our previous discussion on immortality. I ask her the question I ask all artists, "Why do you paint?" She admits the real impetus is most likely existentialist, then adds, "I paint because I am trying to find something that is not apparent yet. Every single time I sit down to paint something, I go in, hoping that I will be surprised—and renewed. And it works every time."

Yet Martha is not an artist who uses art as therapy. She has treated painting as her equal, as her companion, and, for the last two decades, as she puts it, they "have hung in there together."

Things I've Seen

A couple in their twilight years waltzing to a stranger coaxing sugar from an evening violin.

People napping.

A pregnant woman heading to the mainland to have her baby.

Car alarms going off.

Strangers strumming guitars together.

A Benedictine nun, in full habit, traveling from Shaw to the Orcas Island Farmer's Market.

Dogs barking impatiently in cars.

People solving jigsaw puzzles.

Kids playing in the wind.

Black cormorants nesting in ferry pylons.

A man hauling lumber in a convertible Karmann Ghia.

Couples imagining their someday home on the islands.

People reading.

Sunsets so luminous everything else drops away.

People lost.

On the Ferry

Women, and girls, and babies, and men wearing pink pussy hats on their way to a march on Friday Harbor.

Two does swimming.

Resident Orca pods grieving.

Car alarms going off.

Floating ukulele jams.

The good souls, in kayaks and boats, protesting the proposed oil pipeline through the Salish Sea.

Dogs waiting patiently in cars.

The ferry writer-in-residence chatting about books.

A bear paddling island to island.

Friends power walking.

Waves cascading over cars on deck.

Kids cranking out last-minute homework on their school commute.

Car alarms going off.

People dreaming.

People found.

Photo credits back of book

LEAVING THE ISLAND
Orcas to Anacortes ferry

Mist-colored knots of sea glass. A moss-clot
cadged from the trail's edge. The truce

fished word by word from beneath the surface
still unspoken. We carry what we found

what we made there. Three days you and I
let the currents direct our course, slept

on cool sand, let woodsmoke flavor us.
What's left? Slow travel over cold water.

Toward home and days ordered by clocks
instead of tides. We watch through salt-scarred

windows, hoping the dark shapes will rise
beside us, will grace us. We know too well

what can't be willed, only missed
if we look away too soon.

— Elizabeth Austen, Washington State Poet Laureate, 2014-16

ŌDE 39

"
THE ODDS
ARE GOOD
BUT THE GOODS
ARE ODD
"

ISLAND QUOTE ON DATING

HEARTH

HAUTE HAND ME DOWNS

Island-born Kiyomi wears used clothing from Sequel and The Exchange in these photos captured in Sara's Garden, beneath a bower of blooming hops and in the shadow of a century-old homestead house repurposed now as a chapel by the sea.

Our island does not have shopping malls, let alone a boutique for teens. Instead, they share clothing more than their mainland peers; they visit The Exchange to stuff as many donated clothing items as they can fit into a bag for a mere $10; or they shop for homecoming dresses at Sequel, where Keri Lago accepts their old clothes in exchange for credit to help them buy hand-me-downs from others. And, if they can't afford to spend anything at all? Not a problem. Girls can set up a confidential shopping appointment with Dawn Parnell, founder of the not-for-profit Charlotte's Closet. In a private safe space, she will help them find something to wear that makes them feel amazing—for free.

Photo Essay by Peter Lin Carrillo
of Coventry Automatik

APRIL MORNING

The light
comes earlier now.
It comes in and sees
what should not be seen.
Perhaps this is why
it remains so quiet,
so steady. It opens
all the drawers
of day, the tidy ones
and the ones that have been
rummaged over and over
again. It opens the latches
of leaves, the blinds
of sorrow, the lockets
of dew. It opens the hook
and eye
of waking, all the little
snaps
of agony, desire, hope.
I am amazed
at its tolerance.

— Laurel Rust

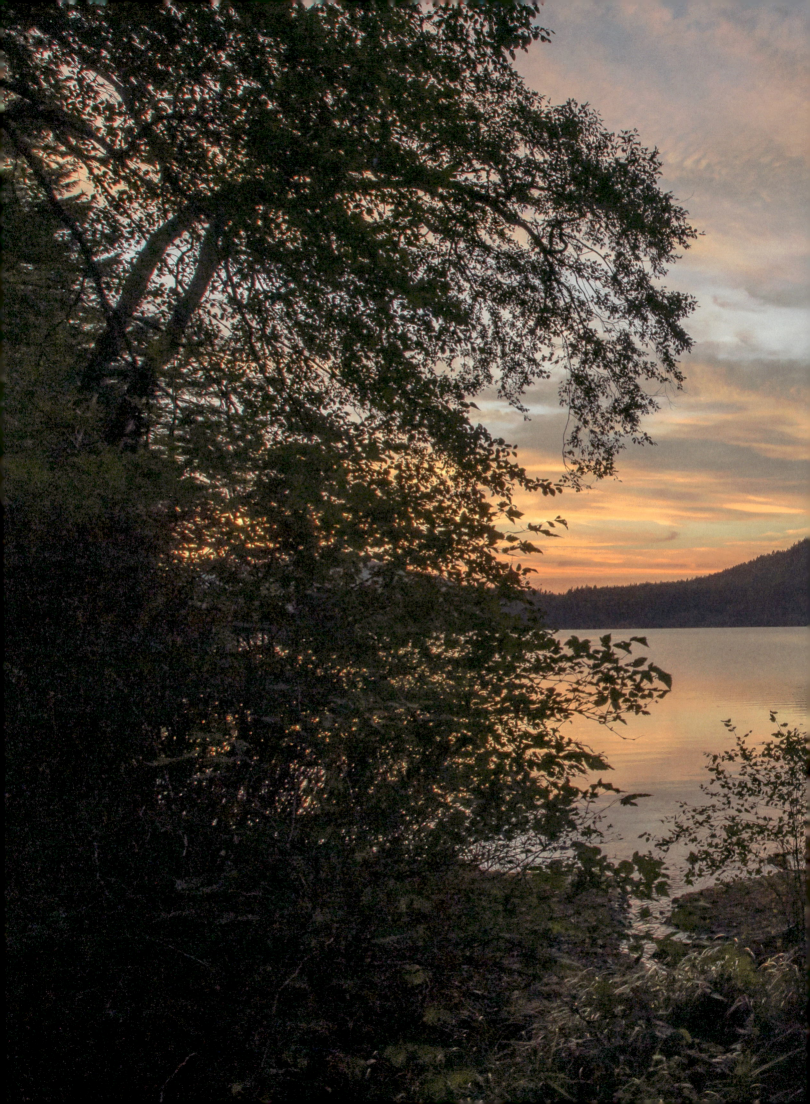

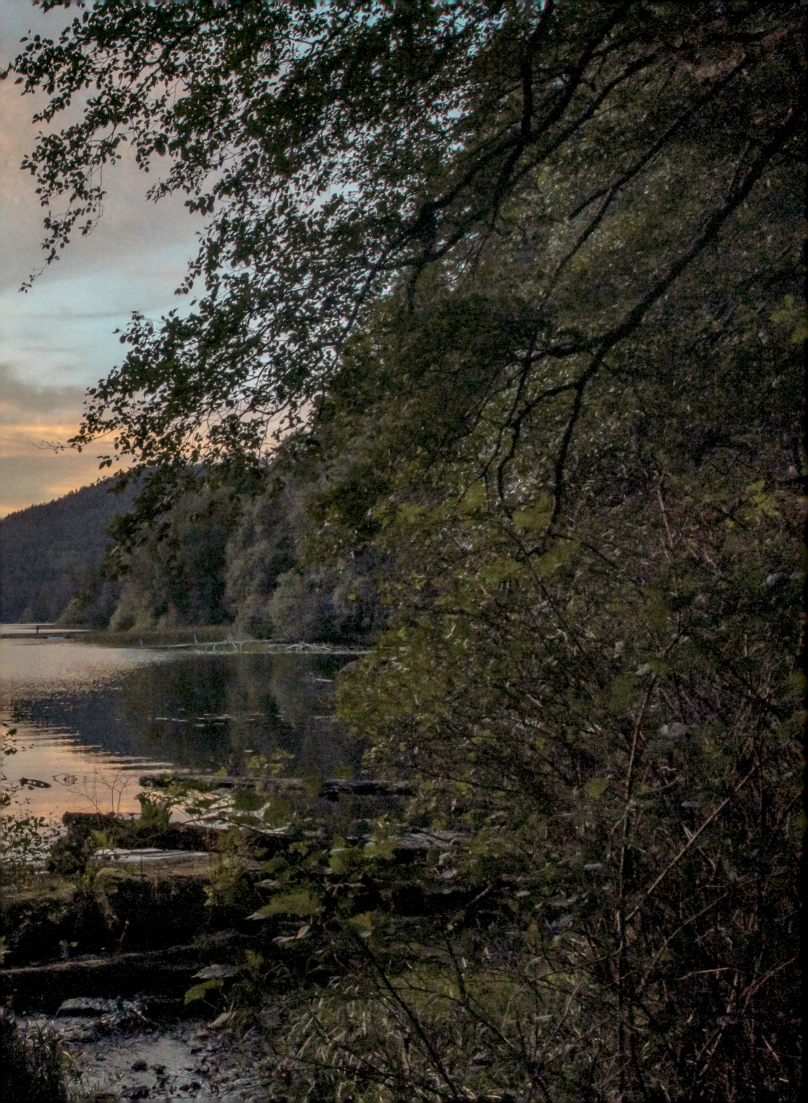

IN THIS LAND, EVERYTHING

is my mother. The mahonia berry
and dogwood blossom, swordfern
and fen. She taught me taxonomy,
showed me shape so I could find her
after her death, burgeoning
in trillium and salal
tadpole and fawn lily,
bursting in a puffball of spores
everywhere, everywhere.

— Poem by Jill McCabe Johnson

Photos by Dennis DeHart

ODE 58

48.6412
122.7810

DOE BAY, ORCAS ISLAND

ODE 62

Words by Theresa Marl | Photographs by Ilias Schneider

There are many books on how to build a treehouse, but none of them warn you that things will not go as planned. You must be willing to start over again and again. And, above all else, you must trust your instincts.

How to Build a Treehouse

1 It is important to find strong trees to support your treehouse. You know this because when you were a child, you spent many hours cradled in the bows of a cedar tree. You don't think about how much you loved that tree when you and your husband first head out into the forest in search of trees. You only know it's a good idea to build a treehouse for your two boys.

Your husband will assess trees based on their size and spacing between one another. You'll consider the wind that whips across the Salish Sea, causing treetops to forever lean back, even when the air is still. You'll have requirements based on fear disguised as opinions—the trees must grow away from the cliff's edge, the trunks must be healthy, the ground must be level. Cedars, we're looking for cedars, you'll tell your husband.

2 Once you have found the perfect cluster of cedars, make a sketch of your treehouse. Review your sons' wish lists: an escape hatch door, windows, a deck, a sleeping loft. Cringe when your husband promises all of it. Know that he'll show you over and over again what's possible when you combine hard work and love (and you let yourself dream a little).

Sit on the edge of a support beam and dangle your feet over the scaffolding in the glow of a full moon. Remember dancing with your husband who doesn't dance because that's the magic of Orcas Island where you met each other in 1994, where he asked you to marry him as you both looked across Doe Bay to the cove where you'll build your house twenty years later and raise your boys. You wanted to rush the process back then, too, but you'll learn that you must build a sound foundation before you can work on the interior.

3 You'll think this was all for your boys until you discover it was not. You will find yourself in the treehouse, your head in the clouds, scratching away in your notebook while your children are at school, pausing to look out at the grove of cedars, to lean into words that have been waiting so long for you to write them. You'll feel as if you've come full circle—returning to Orcas Island, returning to being cradled by forest trees, returning to that little girl you once were. You'll marvel that you found her again after all these years because until now you thought she was lost to you. This is the magic of building a treehouse. Hard work. Love. Dreaming in treetops. And, a place to find yourself again and again. —TM

THE KIDS ARE ALRIGHT...

Here's to the inspirers. The teachers. The coaches. The patrons. The mentors. The ones who see an island kid with talent and say, *oh, yes, you can*. They praise you. Lift you up. Push you forward. They place a pencil in your hand. A microphone to your lips. A stage beneath your feet. Whether you want to change the whole world or just your world, they know you'll have a better chance with one more believer by your side.

The five teens pictured right are all practicing their art at a professional level and they would like to thank a few of the mentors and organizations that have created unique opportunities for them to hone their craft.

(Left to Right)
Cailin Tucker, novelist, Christian School, thanks Novel Lab and Orcas Island Lit Fest

Aristotle Luna, dancer, home-schooled, thanks Anthony The Dancer & Island Inspiration All-Stars, Maria Bullock & Island Aerial Acrobatics, and Dustin Fox & Orcas Island Capoeira

Gray Gailey, editor-in-chief *Wondermint Kids/Girl Folk*, Orcas Island Public School, thanks The Funhouse, *Orcas Issues*, Novel Lab, and Orcas Island Film Fest

Stormy Hildreth, singer, Salmonberry/Spring Street, thanks Grace McCune, Jake Perrine, and Martin Lund

Matthew Laslo, magician, home-schooled, thanks *Orcas Has Talent*, John Mount & Ingrid McClinton (Sea View Theatre), and Willie Thomas

COCOON
Co'coon | \kə kun

Interview by Ayn Gailey | Photographs by Gray Gailey

Sharon Ho and Christa Smith of *Felt + Ceramics* studio are proof that dedication to and reverence for a chosen material leads to profound artisanship. Christa, a longtime islander, who has been spinning and dyeing wool since her early twenties, found felting in her late thirties and began sculpting the material without the use of stitching. Sharon is an artist working with ceramics, photography, and assemblage, initially in Singapore before making the decision to live on Orcas Island eight years ago. Although they barely knew each other five years ago, Sharon and Christa admired each other's work and were inspired by the idea of opening a shared workspace on what they called "a whim."

That whim has led Sharon and Christa to create a series of stunning works at *Felt + Ceramics* studio, where hundreds of visitors have had the opportunity to observe their process and view their work in person. When Ōde co-founder, Sara Farish, and I sat down to conceive this book, we dreamed of having these two artists and friends collaborate on a project to highlight in these pages. Their unique and visually alluring exhibit, COCOON, was birthed from that idea and is the first time they've collaborated on a specific theme. We stopped by their studio on a rainy Friday morning to chat about their new collection.

ŌDE: A cocoon can mean so many things to so many different people. I have an inexplicable fear of moths, so for me, a cocoon can be a frighteningly claustrophobic proposition.

SHARON: The symbolism of the cocoon [and the chrysalis] has rich relevance at many different stages of our lives. For me, personally, it's not scary, but has to do with the unknown and giving up control to that unknown.

CHRISTA: I think it also represents the process of going inward to shed layers and find potential. A unique individual expression that is newly manifested. In a sense, our island environment allows for this.

SHARON: We had asked a lot of people about what Orcas Island meant to them when we were contemplating creating works for *Ōde*. When people described living here, they used phrases like: in a bubble, protected, sheltered, a new start… What I sensed was that many people come here and see the chance to reinvent themselves or transform their lives.

CHRISTA: That's what sparked the idea. So much of the process for these pieces was about transforming the original material, adding layer upon layer to discover or invent something, then removing some of those layers to create the metamorphosis you want.

ŌDE: What a fantastic metaphor for life.

CHRISTA: I totally agree. The cocoon really is a perfect symbol for personal process and growth.

ŌDE: Supposedly, a caterpillar actually disintegrates in its cocoon, but all its essence remains there. That essence then transforms into a moth or butterfly. So many fellow islanders and artists describe destroying things from their past to find their new selves.

SHARON: We also have a protective quiet on this island that can be important to the artistic process.

ŌDE: As you brought up earlier, the letting go of control can be transformative, especially in art. Although to what degree one should let go, the balance of control or thinking vs. feeling, is something that all artists constantly battle.

SHARON: As a ceramicist, I accept that I can't really totally control the clay. I know the form that I'm heading for, but I never know exactly where I'm going. It's literally nothing but mud in front of me. After I play with it, shape it, I put it in the kiln, and the intense heat vitrifies it, transforms it once again. But honestly, whatever comes out of the kiln is always a surprise to me. I will never be able to completely predict the outcome.

CHRISTA: What I love about working with textiles, especially felted wool, is that the way I perceive a piece constantly changes…to the point that sometimes I'll take a previous piece and add more layers to transform it into something else entirely.

ŌDE: Sharon, I love that you have these unexpected stitches incorporated into some of your ceramics for this collection and how that addition is perceived in so many different ways by people. I saw them as sutures, keeping things together. Most likely because a loved one recently had to get stitches.

SHARON: My mom was a seamstress in Singapore, so I've always been drawn to sewing. I love that the stitching has evoked a visceral reaction from people who've seen them.

ŌDE: Do you think that working in a dedicated studio, especially one in the heart of Eastsound, has elevated your art?

SHARON: Absolutely. Having space is freedom.

CHRISTA: I was working out of my home before with kids, and that was such a challenge. On a practical level, a studio allows me to do more. On another level, it inspires me to focus on my art. Sharing a studio space with another artist keeps me inspired and I love seeing how our works play off of each other.

ŌDE: Your studio is an open one. What's it like to create art as locals or strangers mill about you?

SHARON: I enjoy interacting with people who walk in, and I appreciate their questions. My favorite thing is hearing the personal stories that are prompted by the art in our studio. There was a Waldorf teacher who said one of my ceramics reminded her of a song from her childhood, and she proceeded to sing it. Recently, a man played his harmonica for me. I even had a customer who was moving off-island leave me Persian jewelry that he hoped I could incorporate into my art someday.

CHRISTA: A few years ago, another islander brought me medicinal mushrooms known as Turkey Tail. It took me two years, but I found a way to incorporate them in my piece entitled: *Night Whisper*.

SHARON: It's inspiring and reassuring when people interact with the art. That means at the very least that they are having a reaction to it, it moves them. And that moves us.

Detail: *Night Whisper,* wool felt, driftwood, mushroom, ecoprint, plus linen thread.

Photo by Robert Dash

KOMOREBI:
The way sunlight shines through trees

Ayame Bullock

Artist Ayame Bullock's work reminds us to take a moment to slow down and instills a sense of quiet joy and ritual in the everyday.

Ayame Bullock's journey with ceramics began on island in an intensive class with master ceramicist Mary Jane Elgin and a handful of other islanders. "Growing up on a farm and in gardens meant that working with clay was a natural progression for me as an artist," Bullock shares.

She works best when grounded to the land around her, and that groundedness is tangible in her ceramics. Even the work she describes as her "loud" work—gorgeous matte black teapots and bowls that are a departure from her monochromatic white and cream pieces—tends to still be quiet. She's drawn to quiet, and that is evidenced by the rustic one-room cabin she lives in on the Bullock family's multi-generational permaculture homestead. And, while many residents flee for warmer climates come December, Ayame finds her creative zone, reflecting the stillness and quiet of winter in her work.

Ayame initially focused on painting in art school but was drawn to practicing the art of ceramics to calm herself and to regenerate after experiencing adrenal fatigue. She found her style and voice almost immediately. The slow process of hand-building ceramics coaxed her to focus on subtle details and to craft each piece with intention. The result is a stunning balance between rustic and refined. Working with clay also met the rule she has for all art she practices: it has to suit her physical body and her emotional space.

On the horizon, Ayame envisions returning to designing jewelry and painting in her newly built studio. No matter what she chooses to create, Ayame tells us that her work will continue to be inspired by personal experiences, her Japanese heritage, and working surrounded by the serene beauty of the San Juan Islands.

Girl Meets Dirt Founder and Head Jam Maker Audra Lawlor in the plum trees | Photo by Amber Fouts

The Arc of Taste

The arc of taste is long
And slow. From seed
to stem to leaf

from flower to fruit
Plucked or fallen at one's feet
To berries bursting from the vine

Birds and bees stick and give
La petite mort of a longer life yet

Even wind, like sex, casts seed about

So nature's power spreads this way
Like love: A bounty and a feast

Full of rapture in the flush
When not drought in the west
Nor flood in the east

So goes this life of mine

Consume it fast, the mouth whispers
Or dare to let it rot on the vine

From Tree to Table
An old orchard cocktail

Amidst the remnants of a one hundred and thirty-year-old private orchard overlooking Judd Cove, friends Tara Anderson & Michael Cleveland and Carie DeRuiter & Charles West, meet to pluck several varieties of heirloom apples.

The apple trees are leftover from a bygone era, which, at its height in 1907, had Orcas Island exporting 3 million pounds of apples a year to Seattle. Forty-two varieties were grown here, and not one of them is in today's commercial crop.

Carie and Charles' Orcas Island Distillery only presses apples from the islands to distill their award-winning brandy. And, cocktail enthusiasts, Tara and Michael, proprietors of the charming pub and literary hub known as The Barnacle, are partial to it.

For our *Ōde* readers (that's you), they experimented with their handcrafted bitters and shrubs, finally landing on the original recipe you see on the following pages.

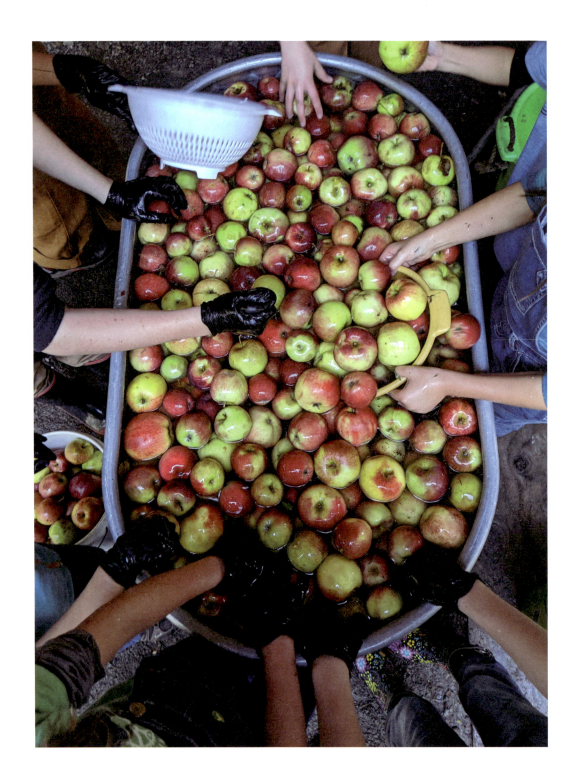

Ode

An old orchard cocktail

2 oz Orcas Island Distillery Apple Brandy
1 raw organic sugar cube*
Dash apple tree bitters*
Fresh rosemary sprig and apple slice as garnish

The Barnacle makes their own apple tree bitters, but you can substitute with Girl Meets Dirt Old Dames Orchard Tree Bitters at home.

Substitute a bar spoon of maple syrup for the raw sugar for a sweet boozy dessert version.

Pairs nicely with warm homemade apple tart or pie.

1. Place a sugar cube in the bottom of an old fashioned glass
2. Add one heavy dash of bitters
3. Once the sugar absorbs the bitters, add the apple brandy
4. Stir sugar until it dissolves
5. Add single large ice cube
6. Bend rosemary sprig over the glass to release oils
7. Stir the drink with the rosemary and rub rim of glass with sprig
8. Garnish with apple slice and rosemary

EASTSOUND is the heart of Orcas Island. Standing at the corner of Main Street & North Beach Road, we took the time to get to know a few locals. For more of their stories and other profiles, visit odeislove.com.

ANGELA DOUGLAS

Angela Douglas is the owner of Orcas Athletics & CrossFit and is a SAFE San Juans advocate. She moved to Orcas from New Orleans in the summer of 2006. She likes to visit the village for a sense of community, art, food, and, of course, the wine.

TREVOR A. WELFORD

Originally from Scotland, Trevor Welford has lived on island for 10 years. He walks 4 to 10 miles every day and has never driven a car. He lives in relative solitude, so he visits town to relieve his hunger for humanity.

NONI

Noni, the 2019 Mayor of Eastsound, is a spry 15-year-old Daschund who was elected on the campaign platform of affordable treats. Noni received 51k votes, helping to raise $108,288 for the non-profit Orcas Island Children's House. Photographed here with campaign manager Dave Roberts.

JIM BREDOUW

Jim Bredouw, founder of The Funhouse, is a musician/composer known for writing the music to Nike's most iconic ad campaigns. He first visited Orcas in 1966 from Bainbridge Island, where he roomed with islander and bandmate Martin Lund before marrying wife Anne. He visits Eastsound regularly to support Orcas Center.

HAZEL MCKENZIE

Hazel McKenzie, 10, was born and raised on Orcas Island. She is both a published writer and fashionista, who has read at literary festivals and can be seen hanging out with friends at the Orcas Island Public Library in town.

DAVID ELLERTSEN & LEE HORSWILL

David Ellertsen and Lee Horswill moved from Las Vegas in 2013. They survived their car plunging into the sea and resulting injuries to open Brown Bear Baking on schedule with the help of their new island employees and friends. They begin most days in Eastsound at their bakery at 5 a.m.

MONA & ISABELLA EVANS

Twins Mona (future politician) & performing artist Isabella Evans, 15, have lived on island their entire lives and in OPAL housing for most of that time. They lobby on and off-island for affordable housing and often visit Eastsound, with or without their dog Risha, to hang out with friends.

CINDY MORGAN

Originally from Puyallup, Washington, Cindy Morgan moved to Orcas in 1980 when there were only 1,500 residents. She opened the Nest Floral Boutique and gift shop in 2004 and visits the village most days to arrange flowers for the shop or special events.

JOE COHEN

Joe Cohen, a financial advisor, first visited Orcas in 1950 when he was two. It was also the first time he met the love of his life, Martha Farish. Reunited on Orcas decades later, they eventually married and made the move from San Diego in 2005. Joe walks to the village every day to meet people, attend board meetings, or do good deeds.

FRANK & JAN LOUDIN

Frank, 89, an illustrator, and Jan, 85, a former escrow manager, have been happily married 61 years despite Frank's pickup line: "Tell me, Jan, how many words a minute do you type?" They moved from Catalina Island in 1990 and visit Kathryn Taylor Chocolates 3 days a week to meet and laugh with friends.

MELINDA MILLIGAN

Director and performing artist, Melinda Milligan, moved to Orcas Island in 1973. As a midwife, she assisted in the delivery of over 1,400 babies on the San Juan Islands. She likes to visit the Lower Tavern in Eastsound for an occasional beer and to perform with the Olga Symphony.

STEPHEN FAIRWEATHER

Stephen Fairweather is a music composer/performer/producer who moved to the island in 2017. He comes to the village to work at New Leaf and be with "his people," the cast and crew of Orcas Center performances. Glitter is his friend.

SAMUEL W. GAILEY

Samuel W. Gailey was raised in a small Pennsylvania town of 400. He lived in Los Angeles for 20 years before moving with his family to Orcas in 2016. A novelist, he's also the co-founder of the free teen writing workshop Novel Lab. He visits the village every morning to write dark things.

JENNY PEDERSON

Jenny Pederson started visiting Beach Haven as a kid in the '60s and made the permanent move to Orcas from Seattle in 1984. She has owned and operated Darvill's Bookstore for the last 35 years. She visits Eastsound almost every day to sell books, organize author events, and chat with locals.

MADDIE OLSEN

Maddie Olsen, an assistant teacher at the Montessori School and a weekend barista at Darvill's Bookstore, lived in Colorado and Seattle before moving to Orcas in 2018. She makes the rounds in the village to attend the theatre and sing karaoke at the Lower Tavern.

ALANNA LAGO

Alanna Lago, 16, moved to Orcas Island from Renton, Washington, fifteen years ago. She plays volleyball, basketball, softball, and oboe. She likes to visit Eastsound to hang with friends and admire the plants at the Nest.

JOANIE RORABAUGH

In 1983, Joanie Rorabaugh made the move to Orcas Island from the state of Maine, and opened Crescent Beach Kayak Rental in 1992. She generally comes into Eastsound every day on her daily walk.

DIANE BERRETH

Diane Berreth moved from D.C. 13 years ago with a Doctorate in Education Leadership and Policy (Special Education). She visits Eastsound to volunteer at the public library, to meet with her Somber Sisters book club, and to serve on the boards of the Orcas Island Community Foundation and the Orcas Community Resource Center.

BLOOD & BONE

"It is the living that turn and chase the dead. The long bones and skulls are tumbled from their shrouds, and words like stones thrust into their rattling mouths."
—Hillary Mantel, *Wolf Hall*

Walking into the first solo exhibit of Kate Geddes' work in Susan Mustard's new Eastsound gallery was life-affirming. That experience paralleled the experience of setting foot on Orcas for the first time. Everywhere you turned, you found yourself in awe of what unexpected beauty nature had woven at that particular moment. In the case of Kate's exhibit, it was explosive color on display, and evocative (wo)manmade beauty being shared with us. More than that, it was Kate's soul, maybe even a glimpse of her lives past, rendered for us.

Kate Geddes works in the realm of mythology. Her larger-than-life paintings include representations of monkeys (mind), martyrs (spirit), mummies (body), and now goddesses. They begin as powerful symbols that represent something profoundly personal and cathartic to Kate, but by painting's end they represent something more universal. While her work is wildly original, Kate explains that the "mystical and bold emotionalism of Goya, Grunewald, and Bacon" inspires her. "They portray startling, shocking images, yet they have great tenderness and beauty," she adds. "It is this tradition to which I wish to add my voice."

And, so she has added her voice, a strong and complete one at that. Although Kate's work is practically an island-kept secret, it won't be for long. It's easy for one to imagine her work hung next to Francis Bacon's in New York's MOMA or London's Lefevre Gallery. Like the work of the artists that inspire her, Kate's paintings leave a lasting impression that is oftentimes visceral and haunting. Her *Madness* quadriptych (view at odeislove.com), created after a friend went insane, was an exorcism of sorts for her, and a perfect example of her process.

(continued on pg. 100)

On opposite page: *Shroud*, acrylic, charcoal and rice paper 80 x 42

Caught, acrylic, charcoal 41 x 29

Years before Kate ever painted, she would tell friends: "I know I'm a painter." However, with kids to raise and a busy career, she didn't have the energy to paint, but she did have faith that it was only a matter of time. After a long career as a textile artist and clothing designer, which included traveling back and forth to India for decades, her children—she is mother to artist and Springboard owner Libi Geddes and aunt to sculptor Aleph Geddis* who appears in the pages of this book—grew up and at a young sixty-years-old, Kate was accepted to the San Francisco Art Institute. Let it be known though that Kate did not attend art school because she didn't know how to paint; she went because she couldn't draw, and for what she had in mind, drawing was vital.

Shroud, drawn in charcoal and finished with acrylic and rice paper, is part of what Kate refers to as the Bog series, works inspired by the hundreds of mummified human bodies discovered in the raised peat bogs of Northern Europe. These men and women (and a few children) were killed or sacrificed in rituals thousands of years ago, and they have captured Kate's imagination. When she first gazed into the face of a well-preserved bog person on exhibit in the UK, she felt as if she could see their soul. Kate's Celtic Pagan ancestors believed the bogs, half-earth, half-water, and open to the heavens, were a portal to the Otherworld. For her, they represent the mysteries of the shifting borderland between life and death.

Shroud is more subdued than other works in the Bog series; it was created during a period when Kate was seriously ill and was hospitalized for ten days. She had been working on the piece before being admitted to the hospital. "When I was released, and I knew I was going to live, I finished her," Kate shares. That protective cocoon quality of a shroud enveloping her felt like "coming home" to her.

The stunning artwork entitled *Caught* also has a lighter touch than much of Kate's other work. The lone figure in the painting, done with acrylic and charcoal, depicts a figure at once being held but being released, too. According to Kate, the "mystical monkey is often a symbol of human frailty and strength," and in her own paintings, they come to "portray the emotional life and struggles we face in the world." There is always a compelling and cathartic story behind every painting Kate creates, and we are so grateful that this immensely talented and prolific painter has chosen Orcas Island as the place where she shares those stories first.

*Kate changed the spelling of her last name

View more of Kate Geddes' work and hear a conversation with her about her art at odeislove.com/kategeddes

Old survey stakes spell "Thank You" after the Madrona Point land transfer to the Lummi

THE POWER OF PLACE

Story by Toby Cooper | Photographs by Peter C. Fisher

Madrona Point—Ts'el-xwi-sen'—is the beating heart of Orcas Island. The Lummi have known it for thousands of years, paddling treacherous canoe miles to bring their deceased tribal elders to the sacred place of eternal rest. James Tulloch knew it when, around 1890, he attempted unsuccessfully to block the purchase by the Harrison family, who Tulloch feared would devalue the deep Lummi identity with the land. Norton Clapp knew it when he paid money for a property that he hoped others would pay him more to give up. And, nearly forgotten among the star-power, a thoughtful and intimate friend to William Randolph Hearst II named "Nancy," knew it—but let us not get ahead of the story.

"If I go, you go."

Peter Fisher contemplated the sound of those words for a moment, allowing them to soak deep. Part prophecy, part threat, but every ounce a clarion call to action, Peter knew his life was about to change. It surprised him not at all that when he heard those words, he was alone among the trees on Madrona Point.

The year was 1984. "I heard that the point was going to be developed," Peter remarks as if it all happened last Tuesday. "I went out there with my camera, and the land spoke to me of its sacred value to the community. There was no turning back."

But Peter was not alone in his mission. "It was about power and place, and the power of place," he says today. Eventually, that power stretched from Eastsound to Washington, DC, from Peter's study of the Nantucket Land Bank to the halls of Congress, from the San Juan County Council to the elders of the Lummi Nation. In the end, it was the confluence of remarkably synchronized actions by an unlikely collection of complete strangers, all inspired by the undeniable spiritual power of 30 acres of trees.

Some secrets Madrona Point still holds. Long assumed a place of traditional burial, the Lummi historians hold that the bodies of their most revered ancient elders were elevated into the trees (actually *in* their canoes), where weather and scavengers and time itself would render them back to the earth.

Now, as then, the big firs stand erect and proud, like diplomats at a reception, drinks in hand, exchanging imperceptible nods of recognition. They converse in low tones, wishing for rain but remaining unperturbed when there is none. Pallid bark etched by storms, yearly cone crops adored by squirrels, they ask nothing more than to be left alone on the timeless shores of the Salish Sea.

But the sylvan Madrona's grab all the attention. Since the groves of fir beat them to the best ground, they reach sideways for sunlight over the salty rocks at the water's edge. They are the unruly group at the kids' table. Their improbable, perpetually peeling red and green trunks twist about in a riot of movement that mocks the stately firs. And yet, it is their essential beauty that inspires memory, passion, and action.

Listening to the land in 1984, Peter's first and ultimately pivotal act was to create a magnificent 28-foot collapsible accordion-style rendition of his best Madrona Point photographs, published in a single uber-limited run of seven hand-crafted volumes, on premium sale for $2500 each. The book became an inspirational symbol of the wider campaign to save the point, including rousing public meetings and hearings, but by September of 1989, the Orcas community faced a classic binary choice, save Madrona Point, or let the laissez-faire economic forces dictate the outcome. Saving the point, of course, meant someone otherwise in line for profit would need to be compensated. And that price tag would be millions.

Odd Fellows Hall, February 17, 1990. *A buoyant Orcas community celebrates the deed transfer with the Lummi Nation. William Randolph Hearst II in attendance.*

The chainsaws were literally poised to snarl. Desperately needed was just one tiny, indispensable link to connect four years of inspired grassroots action on Orcas with the fearsome political potency that is Washington, D.C. Like the light switch on the wall or the neck in the middle of the hourglass, such links are the difference between movement and utter stagnation. Here, that link was Nancy.

With no fanfare or public pretense, Nancy, with the honest passion that Orcas Island seems to inspire in all who step ashore, inspired her good friend William Randolph Hearst II to hastily enroll himself as quarterback of the effort. Hearst took his mission to heart. He spliced the visual impact of Peter's remarkable accordion book with the unstoppable energy of the Orcas community, hopped a flight to Washington, D.C., and in remarkably efficient fashion won unanimous Congressional approval for a $2.2 million Interior Department appropriation to buy Madrona Point, transfer title and management rights to the Lummi and set in place a timeless conservation mandate to protect the fragile forested point.

Madrona Point still speaks. The land reminds us daily that we—the Lummi, the county councilmembers, the gaggle of summer tourists, all of us—are not owners but guests on this green Earth. When we work together, we can accomplish great things—Peter reminds us that our community's passion for saving the point led directly to the formation of two lasting and respected island institutions, the San Juan County Land Bank and the OPAL Community Land Trust. Only if we listen to the land and to each other do we enjoy such winnings. And then only if we live lightly enough so as not to upset nature's foundational underpinnings that permit us to remain do we give ourselves the chance to win.

The beating heart of Orcas Island speaks to all who stop to hear its call.

Editor's Note: Today, Madrona Point is again at a crossroads. Faced with vandalism and homeless camps, the Lummi recently closed the point to all public access. When, in 1989, Hearst spoke eloquently of the need to "preserve the environmental integrity of Madrona Point and to establish . . .cross-cultural cooperation," the resulting legislation called for the potential establishment of a cultural visitor center. That vision has yet to be fulfilled, but the Orcas community has not forgotten. The land brought us together those many years ago and it seems likely to do so again.

Photos by Peter Lin Carrillo

WOMAN IN THE WOODS

There is so much raw beauty on this remote island of ours that it's easy to understand why people are lured here. Why people stay is a more complex matter, and the answer to that question is often more profound.

"I could cry," are the first words Michell "Mitch" Marshall speaks when she sits down to discuss her life and the inspiration behind Woman in the Woods, the non-profit arts organization that she founded in 2017. "It has been an emotional journey, with a lot of painful experiences," she admits, "but if I had to do it all over again, pain included, I would do it in a heartbeat."

"I had the most wonderful, intense, childhood," is how Mitch describes growing up in Boulevard Park, a small town eight miles south of Seattle, then Burien. She doesn't remember ever seeing another black family in the community, but she does remember kids throwing rocks at her because of the color of her skin. As she shares the stories of her childhood, it's clear that to truly understand why Mitch is such a positive force, one must first get to know her father, Charles Silicious Woods.

Charles, an engineer at Boeing and a bass-baritone for the Seattle Madrigal Society, loved opera, played piano and held musical salons in the family's living room. He and Mitch's mom, Ophelia, exposed Mitch and her three sisters to art from an early age, which was not the norm. One of her strongest memories is of her dad, using the nickname that only he used, telling her: "Shorty, you're going to have to be better than everyone else because they're going to expect you to be mediocre." He was preparing Mitch for a lifetime of prejudice, and she took it to heart.

Charles taught the kids in their neighborhood to play piano and, like the Mitch we know, when he thought he could improve something in the community, he did. "My dad took it upon himself to start a petition to get a stoplight installed at a busy corner of 136th street in Burien after several car accidents happened there. When he was visiting neighbors to get their signatures, one of them told him, "You know, there's another petition going around. It's to get you out of the neighborhood." I don't know what happened with that petition, but my dad's petition got us a stoplight that still remains today, and people long referred to it as the Charles Woods Light."

I always knew the art I wanted to bring to the island would not be easy. The most moving art is born out of blood, sweat, and tears, and sometimes that can be hard for an audience, but hard can be so uplifting.

As an adult, Mitch was happy to discover Orcas Island. When she saw the rustic hamlet of Olga for the first time, it reminded her of the best parts of her childhood, and she felt "deeply comfortable." In 2007, her husband Doug retired as a corporate attorney, she gave up her job in finance at Microsoft, and they made the permanent move to Orcas Island, where they bought the 40-year-old Office Cupboard, and they built their home in West Sound. However, after settling in, Mitch experienced the feeling that nothing had really changed. "People would walk into the shop and remark on the color of my skin," she explains. There was no maliciousness, but a frustrating level of ignorance and insensitivity. There was a focus, sometimes unconscious, sometimes not, on how she didn't fit in rather than how she did.

"I actually thought about leaving the island," she confesses. "I was walking around Mountain Lake, not another soul around, contemplating what I should do. I knew I would miss the sheer beauty and the serenity of the island, and that saddened me. As I made my way through the cedars, I decided that I could make the island feel more like my home, too. I will add to the beauty, I thought. With each step, the more I came to believe that I could change the social landscape. By the time I reached my car, the vision had crystallized. I was going to use performance art to start a conversation—a powerful one."

Mitch finished her three-year term as President of the Orcas Island Chamber of Commerce and threw herself into the creation of Woman in the Woods with Doug, and a board led by president Norm Stamper, a retired Seattle Police Chief, and fellow lover of the arts.

Since then, the mission has been to seek and promote a better understanding and appreciation of racial and cultural differences through various forms of artistic expression. Woman in the Woods has hosted Poetry Grand Slam champion Alex Dang; Blackbird, a genre-jumping collaboration with Marc Bamuthi Joseph and Daniel Bernard Roumain; and Guggenheim Fellow, cellist and artist Paul Rucker.

When faced with what was lacking on our remote island, when it may have been easier to simply leave, Mitch chose to stay—to make a positive difference. It's that indomitable modern pioneer spirit and determination that adds a rare kind of beauty that other isolated communities lack. Woman in the Woods shows are avant-garde and wildly entertaining, but you also spend part of the time with a lump in your throat. As Mitch puts it, "I always knew the art I wanted to bring to the island would not be easy. The most moving art is born out of blood, sweat, and tears, and sometimes that can be hard for an audience, but hard can be so uplifting."

Photo by Ilias Schneider

Photo by Kyle Carver

A Ladies Hunting Club

The Ladies Hunting Club of Orcas Island, aka The Huntress Guild, was founded partially as a response to the decimation of wildflowers and pollinators, the declining health of forests and Madrona trees, and an ecological system out of balance. Founders, Samantha Martin, Sommer McKenzie, Xoe Chue, Erika Ekrem, Dana Thompson-Carver, and Amy Vanderwarker banded together in 2019 to learn to hunt deer to promote a healthier deer population, ecological balance, self-reliance and community building. They also hope to feed their families and those in need with wild, local meat.

REQUIREMENTS:
Shotgun, muzzleloader, bow & arrow (highly skilled only)
Must adhere to strict safety codes
Willing to work as a group for a common goal
Deep respect of the deer as an integral part of the island

ACTIVITIES:
Hunter's education & field skill evaluations
Shooting practice
Native plant and wildflower restoration
Hunting and field dressing
Hide preservation and leather tanning
Making crafts from bones and hides
Venison recipe sharing

LAND ACKNOWLEDGMENT:
We live in unceded Coast Salish territory

INCLUSIVITY:
Welcome to ALL, including those who identify as Beings of Color, Non-Binary, Gender Queer, LGBTQA, and, yes, *men.*

To participate in a civil discussion on the activities of the Huntress Guild of Orcas Island, visit odeislove.com

PACKING FOR PEACE
By Jill McCabe Johnson

After Matt Hohner's "How to Unpack a Bomb Vest"

i.	ii.
when you say you're packing	fill your bags with dandelion seeds
carrying	the stuff of wishes
armed	you can launch
loaded for bear—I want to believe	in the wind—cram feathers and the taste
you're carrying	of wild strawberries
a kind of mettle	into pockets
facing fear	of torn memories
with friendship	palm the scent of lilac
maybe a nest of	pine-sap spikemoss
hummingbird eggs	and hollowed out cedar
filled with marvels	offer these to strangers
peace requires so much more than	the unspent
weapons and	promises the
explosive	blossoming
shells	of dreams

Photo by ACG

ORCAS ISLAND MIXTAPE

Adam Farish, music producer and co-founder of the 8-Stem app, shares an eclectic mix of songs written or recorded on Orcas Island.

KATIE GRAY
Set Free

SEA STARS
You and Me

THE BURNED
(featuring Katie Gray)
Time

THE BHAJANS
Jay Ambe

1020 POINT LAWRENCE
Phase Dance

LULACRUZA
Uno Resuena

THE BURNED
Undertaker

BLETCHLEY PARK PROJECT
The Now Song

MANDY TROXEL
One Year Ago Today

PERLO
Patterns

HENRI BARDOT
Make You Love Me

MREE
When You Come Home

BRUCE HARVIE
Leave Me Alone or I'll Find Someone Who Will

SUSAN OSBORN
Makin' the Two One

MARTIN LUND
Misty Meadow/March Morning

CHRISTOPHER PEACOCK
& GENE NERY
Joy to the World

HENRI BARDOT
Dreaming is Dangerous

LUKA PALISÆDE
Treading Water

Listen to all songs on Spotify

Photo by Kyle Carver

48.3725
122.5957

DEER HARBOR, ORCAS ISLAND

Sculptor Aleph Geddis

Words by Forect Eckley | Photos by AJ Ragasa

The visionary sculptures of Aleph Geddis integrate sacred forms of geometry with traditional hand carving techniques. Aleph grew up on Orcas Island apprenticing with his stepfather, Walter Henderson, a master woodworker. Through traveling and collaborating with other artists he has developed his own understanding of form and means of expression. Now, Aleph splits his time between his studio in Bali and his family's carving shed on Orcas Island, where we spoke with him about the influence of travel, the difference between his life in Bali and Orcas, and the how spirituality and creativity interrelate.

"After apprenticing with my dad and then leaving, I slowly found my own voice. Now, when I come back to Orcas I can bring different information and other artists who can also share and evolve the culture and now different kinds of art are being done here which is kind of magical. The difference between being here and being in my studio in Bali is that when I'm on Orcas, I won't leave the property for a week or two weeks at a time. Whenever I think about building new creative spaces, I wonder if they will have the same magic and openness as this studio. A huge part of what makes this place special is Walter's focus and the intention he has. This has always been a place where Walter would drop anything he is working on to help someone else with their project so it has this quality of sharing and openness to it that naturally facilitates creativity. The culture of it is so strong that motivation here is often automatic... When I'm on Orcas I wake up and I just start creating. There are not many places like that."

"Keeping a beginner's mindset is another big thing in my spiritual practice and in my work... when I go into a new environment it helps me look at my work in a fresh way and that's a key part of my creative process. I've been creating these little creative pockets in different places. I can achieve the feeling of being somewhere new, and at the same time I can be focused and productive."

"I started out doing a lot of power-carving while I was apprenticing with my dad. It required a lot of detail work and machined kind of stuff... and you know... it was always very dusty and noisy. From there, I gravitated towards doing more work with hand tools. With hand tools it's all about the process and being present and that led me to carving as my spiritual practice because it centers me. I can focus on being present with the chip and just focus on the quality of the chip. My work feels like a Taoist or Zen practice. So, whenever I'm too much in my head, carving brings me back and connects me again. With the work, you have to be into the process. When you are present, the work always turns out to be better than if you are constantly focused on the end result."

Charolais cows at Driftwood Ranch, established by Charles Arnt in 1960. Photo by Peter C. Fisher

OCTOBER, DRIVING TO WORK
by Laurel Rust

The morning began fine
enough: clocks set
back, it was nearly light
on the drive to work

enough to see the doe
dead beside the road
through Crow Valley, her black eyes
open as stones beneath water.

The straightaway, afterwards,
seemed far too long, miles
and miles until the curve, until
the steam rising off the backs
of Charolais
grazing their pasture, the sun
to their knees, still rising.

Olympic Lodge, Deer Harbor, 1985, Albert Zeman (upper window). On porch, B. Sadie Bailey (L) and David Smith (R).
Photo by Peter C. Fisher

This is an Ode to Life
by Kamand Kojouri

This is an ode to life.
The anthem of the world.
For as there are billions
of different stars
that make up the sky,
so, too, are there billions
of different humans
that make up the Earth.
Some shine brighter
but all are made of the same
cosmic dust.
O the joy of being
in life with all these people!
I speak of differences
because they are there
like the different organs
that make up our bodies.
Earth, itself, is one large body.
Listen to how it howls
when a human
is in misery.
When one kills another,
Earth feels the pangs in its
chest. When one orgasms,
Earth craves a cigarette.

Look carefully,
these animals are freckles
that make Earth's face lovelier
and more loveable.
These oceans are Earth's limpid
eyes. These trees, its hair.
This is an ode to life.
The anthem of the world.
I will no longer speak of
differences, for the similarities
are even greater.
Look closer. There may be distances
between our limbs
but there are no spaces
between our hearts. We long to be one.
We long to be in nature and
run wild with its wildlife.
Let us celebrate life and living,
for it is sacrilegious to be ungrateful.
Let us play and be playful,
for it is sacrilegious to be serious.
Let us celebrate imperfections
and make existence proud of us,
for tomorrow is death,
and this is an ode to life.
The anthem of the world.

COFOUNDERS
Sara Farish & Ayn Gailey

PRODUCTION TEAM
Sara Farish—Layout + Design
Ayn Gailey—Editor-in-Chief
Sarah Cooper—Manager of Minor Miracles
Samuel W. Gailey—Editorial
Gray Gailey—Proofing
Paul Huber—Design Consultant + Mentor

PHOTOGRAPHERS
In order of appearance

Cover credited at front
Peter Lin Carrillo of CoventryAutomatik
Dennis DeHart
Deborah Heffley Jones
Ayn Gailey
Ilias Schneider
Peter C. Fisher
Kyle Carver
Gray Gailey
Robert Dash
Amber Fouts
AJ Ragasa

Ferry snapshots:
[L to R]
Ayn Gailey
Peter O'Brien
Dennis DeHart
Adam Farish
Deborah Heffley Jones
Terri McClary
Deborah Heffley Jones
Gray Gailey
Lila Speed Richardson
Meagan Gable

The poem, *Packing for Peace*, on page 117, originally appeared in *The Tishman Review*.

WRITERS
In order of appearance in book

Ayn Gailey*
Toby Cooper
Jonathan White
Flora Lister
Samuel W. Gailey
Elizabeth Austen
Laurel Rust
Jill McCabe Johnson
Theresa Marl
Forest Eckley
Kamand Kojouri

*All unattributed stories, words, and photos by Ayn Gailey

THANK YOU
San Juan County Lodging Tax Grant
Orcas Open Arts
Darvill's Bookstore
Hemlock Printers
Robin Lee Carlson
Carla Stanley (handwriting embellishments)
Outlook Inn and Water's Edge
Orcas Island Distillery
The Barnacle
Adam Farish
Forest Eckley & Glasswing
Christa Smith, Paul & Celia Groeninger
Joe Brotherton & Doe Bay Resort
Jude Nash
Jeff and Angie Johnson
Jesica DeHart
Dan Edghill
Donna Laslo
Eric Morris
Kiki Roumel
Sequel Clothing Boutique
Dana Thompson-Carver
Diane White
John Cunningham
Shannon Bindler
Stacey Lancaster
Hemlock Printers
Miranda Otto
Kiyomi

EXPLORE MORE

The Ōde Music Playlist
Festivals + Rituals
Calendar of Events
Full Contributor Profiles
More Conversations & Stories
Behind-The-Scenes Photos
Sketchbook by Robin Lee Carlson

www.odeislove.com

@odeislove

St. Ōde Press prints 100% Carbon Neutral
on Forest-Positive, FSC paper